T0160842

WHITTLING A NEW FACE
IN THE DARK

WHITTLING A NEW FACE
IN THE DARK

DJ DOLACK

Black Ocean
Boston · New York · Chicago

To reprint, reproduce, or transmit electronically or by recording all or
part of this manuscript, beyond brief reviews or educational purposes,
please send a written request to the publisher at:

Black Ocean
P.O. Box 52030
Boston, MA 02205
blackocean.org

Cover illustration by Stefanie Augustine.
www.stefanieaugustine.com

Design and composition by Snack Bar.

ISBN 978-1-939568-02-1

Library of Congress Cataloging-in-Publication Data

Dolack, D. J., 1979–
  [Poems. Selections]
  Whittling a new face in the dark / by DJ Dolack.
    pages ; cm.
  ISBN 978-1-939568-02-1 (alk. paper)
  I. Title.
  PS3604.O42W48 2013
  811'.6--dc23
                                        2013005157

FIRST EDITION

ACKNOWLEDGMENTS

Some of these poems originally appeared in the following journals, courtesy of the editors, to whom the author is extremely grateful: *Diode, Fou, H_NGM_N, Handsome, Sink Review, Verse.*

Several poems from this manuscript also appeared in the chapbooks *No Ser. No.* from the incomparable Greying Ghost Press, and *12 Poems* from Eye For An Iris Press.

EFI is dead; long live EFI.

Thank you to the following who have had great influence on these contents, directly or other. I am forever grateful: my parents Dennis and Camille Dolack, brother Dean, Alison Lee Augustine Dolack, Paige Ackerson-Kiely, Carl Annarummo, Stefanie Augustine, The Augustine Family, John Deming and all at *Coldfront,* Timothy Donnelly, Kate and Max Greenstreet, B. Colby Hamilton, Joshua Harmon, Ian J. Kern, John F. Kersey, Bill Knott, Matthew Lombardi, Mary Ruefle, Peter Jay Shippy, James Leon Zabriskie Suffern, Allison Titus, David Wojahn, Janaka Stucky and the Black Ocean staff: Carrie Adams, Nikkita Cohoon, A. Minetta Gould, editors and publishers of the above journals, anyone who has booked me at a reading, and everyone who's let me put them in front of a camera.

Thank you.

CONTENTS

Alison

It was as if some space had opened up, a little rift, between words and whatever they were supposed to be doing. I stumbled in that space, I fell.

...

I don't mean to exaggerate. I knew what words meant, more or less. A cup was a cup, a window a window. That much was clear. Was that much clear? There began to be moments of hesitation, fractions of a second when the thing I was looking at refused to accept any language. Or rather, between the thing and the word a question had appeared, a slight pause, a rupture.

...

I felt tremendously tired, but also alert. Not to speak, not to form words, not to think, not to smear the world with sentences — it was like the release of a band of metal tightening around my skull.

— Stephen Millhauser, from "History of a Disturbance"

WHITTLING A NEW FACE
IN THE DARK

NYC POSTCARDS

A word falls because I ask of it

The neuronal circuits get established

Because the conjugal bird is much more a bird
when he's solo, born into a world

with worms in the grass, blind
       and tactless

You glance up mid-chapter and loosen
a button no man could subdue

Res extensa; res cogitans

This world has been given its fair chance to avoid us

1

WHAT THEY WANT ME TO TELL YOU

It's one of those things
        that could go on and on.

You might be waiting for someone to return
and it might take half your day,

years of dog-eared pages
on the shelves.

        So far,
today's bowls in the sink.

But I suppose something could happen in there,

the room with so much light.

With your hands, you might
create a space and say

I love you this much

without knowing who it will be.

You might say I love you, for Christ sake —

I love you out through the back window
down the fire escape

to the neighbor's yard,

I love you
how the elderly love bakeries,

in the way they say *cake*.

It's one of those things

you might know a little about —

real eye contact in the mirror, reading
in low light.

People quoting
when their empathy is down;

people marking their lives by epiphanies.

Plainsongs under the breath

when doing those dishes;

Quixotic foreplay.

Night is coming in,

or you are moving towards it.

Sugar granules
under your bare feet, roman candles

in the distance become.

If you'd like to play prison, I'll go out for milk.

You set the table for the sum
of who you think

we should have been by now.

Remember the cattle in the freezer
the onions

and news.

Out in the yard,
the deeply-carved initials let us know

we're not the first version,
so why whittle?

I have given up the service.

So google me.

Tell me what you want —

my envelopes are piling unopened too.

The rain water is filtered;
the doctor is real in.

If I sit up long enough
it becomes mourning;

if I

say abundance, tell me

what do I mean?

JANUARY

The pistol-clean mouth
is oiled and you will marry

next winter.
Here is a winter
a meter, warm

pocketknife dull
in the pocket
for your pearl fingers.

For the pearl-
fingered:
I don't know how

to put this.
Snow showing the air.
A shovel

ripping into
a patch of ice,

hacking through it.
Divisive wind
you don't dare think

has a place. The weight
you carry
until what you ask for

is there: your name
inked on some pulp,

pressed into plastic,
settled into bone

and you look up

and think
these hands
these

hands, and
say it aloud.

I THOUGHT WE DISCUSSED THIS ALREADY

It's going to get better
before it gets worse:

Lovemaking will trail off
under the low-shelf haze,

cottonwood in the air.

The deep
inverted fissures of ceiling

will beg

take light off the room.

The kitchen sink will survive,

but the photos burn like salt.

The scent of bourbon left
on the doorknob

so it will appear

the world is in the hands

of something bigger.

                      Thanks for calling but
we're not here.

If you leave your number

ROT AND POPLAR

We quit when our graffiti
read *vote yes.*

Now our fingerprints
are awry *&*
we'll need at least

some time to deify,
to find our ghost.

Buy us a round
but we won't stick
for discussion;

it's tough
being seen.
We can't talk debacle

& our chemicals
aren't worth
the clatter.

We might slip and
call it *our* winter,
lifting the sutures

from our arms
with false teeth. And you,
you could have told us

that a little might ebb
over the edge is all —

we may have stood
for some dream retention
a scent of fresh catkin

or a good modest lisp
in its song, from its tongue;
around its lips.

FOR: NEVER YOUNG

How the dashboard light gives a little like that

off the cellophane
of my mother's cigarettes

and the dead smell
of smoke in cold air,

that look
in her eyes

like it's always too soon
to see what I've become.

Once, out late
after some holiday, dad saw
what that puppy

could do —

three of us humming along
Rt. 80, beneath us

the contraption vibrating
steadily

and in our teeth.

Grandfather is alone in the yellow house

with the flea market pistol.

And grandmother
in our living room

with the baby to her chest

rocks a little too
violently, asks

please, Jesus. Please

Jesus,

please.

What it's like to know
your monster
doesn't give a fuck.

So much, in fact, he locks eyes
with your grandson
just before.

Sometimes the metaphor
is too good —

So much that it becomes expensive:

the ambulance

spinning its weight
in the mud

while the body bleeds out.

And the boy
playing in the deep tracks

for months
before someone fills them in.

The only child
in many a huddle

of sobbing —

moaning, understood.

The first corpse before you
there, pumped out

and rendered down,

and sutured.

And rendered down.

ORGANIZING HIS MOTHER'S PAPERS

The wooden drawer gasps out
and it's all there grouped
and gathered like that.

The sound of the thing
is a little voiceless harp that doesn't whisper
I coaxed her from one ledge to another.

NYC POSTCARDS

Dawn is a color
I am condemned to describe:

       my mother's penmanship
on the anesthesiologist's forms —

       father holding me
up close to the casket

so I could search
the dead man's temple for an
entry wound. People

       trying hard; people
really trying.

(PLEASE DISENGAGE)

Like a cup of
thick milk

offered minutes after
a downpour on Mt. Pisgah.

Like a pretense
of famine.

My lips gesture

black fields of ice.

HOW A YEAR IS BORN IN QUEENS, NY

Like the curtain letting in
a thick little light,

close though not yet a halo.

There's a nickname up against
the pillowcase; the heater

breathes like,   you know,

sheets up over bodies

now husks.

But when it's all shed,
the meals are rarely what

is asked of them. The tea
is good but, come now,

just ounces of water.

Simply not something to slide
across the brake man's tongue,

and no, not like
a communion at all.

NYC POSTCARDS
(SELF-PORTRAIT WITH MARCH REPRISE)

What's here

and what useless creature
goes around

confirming the world?

I am waiting in the cold
late afternoon sun.

I am thinking of good things to say
first thing in the morning.

My friends know
not to bring up the little

matter of wind,
or when we drink

how the bar room light dims
and the walls come over us

like eyelids
before a bad sleep.

March perched quietly on her stool
thumbs through a copy of that

old elegy.
I want to heave up

my apology,
make her think

there's nothing of me
left in there.

But what's here:

the hidden machines
inside us, churning

what they can.

And I can't recall
whose to-do lists

make up the new issue
of *jubilat,*

how the whole damn birdcage in the corner

swings, but what's next
is sort of tell-tale, not complete:

March on the frozen dock
a few minutes past midnight.

March in the
post-baptismal sheets,

the only announcement
to bare its scalpel.

And sure, if she gestures.

If she finds me

whittling a new face in the dark.

How do I know
she's actually

who I say she is:

She turns to me
says,

I'm buying,

and I don't know how
she means it.

NYC POSTCARDS (FROM UNION HALL)

And whisper here,
here is the problem.

In the bar room
we pour a little water
for palpability.

The notion is one
loose suture

that fingers the liquor;
and our letters are silk, sent
endlessly,

read by the night.
The light is one
obscene gesture:

people who don't
look like their names.

When the letter is sent, he walks the length of the pacing room and waits for word. The night folds backward into the dimming house where the body accrues its memory. There is laughing. The whole exaggerated wish of it going on and on. Some wiring beneath his skin dimly warms. Birds flutter in from the chimney. He finds their feathers have been gnarled by pirate birds who've intercepted and pillaged the words. All of their breath coming at his face in heaves, exalts. He doesn't know what she's received.

ELEGY FOR POETRY'S EFFIGY; ENTROPY

You think it's
a little prayer that staves off

but it's not.

It might be
in the avenue lights,

a ditch try for a woman

under her third
at the bar

as she eyes
the tendress's lefty pour —

The brittle din
of the waiter

slowly organizing utensils, a low

yellow moon outside
sipping back the sky.

Something in the way men
bring home work.

The way you use only one ear for the phone.

A canned scene amidst the laughter.

WHITTLING A NEW FACE IN THE DARK

You have sloughed off
to your death so many times

the fugue lifts and transitions by heart —
the heart's animal

heaves up terrific things and rests
against the ribcage like a fighter been already cut.

(You might be eradicated, slung
upon stone.

Lip marks on the old glass
hold the condensation of night sweats
            and moth belly.)

What's the feeling, what's it they mean

when they tell you to taste victory.

Satisfactory this; satisfactory that.

When you tear-up I put out the perennials.

This is
what's come of

people giving it to people straight.

Unseasonable snow in the tea.

You wait for a phone call
in the only world
worth sifting through fingers.

The New York Headache Center

in its lull.

Point out the coward in me
and I will bring you his head on a matchstick.

There is one satisfied bird crossing over
the porch for the gutter;

and one sitting here,
the only prayer from Catholic school

come back to collect.

Now I'll ask you again, and then I'll go.

WHERE OUR DATA LIVE

On a notion of farms; in
the pines.

In medias res, in dictum;
on the battlefield where the

local and express trains
leapfrog.

In the pines.
In the airbag talcum;

among the phrasals.

Did you want
to jar it, can it

in the late season and hope
it discovers

a love for enclosure?

Develops a sense of taste
over time?

That song
in your head again.

And time is what
brings you back

into the passenger seat after school,
afraid to sing along

to the lyric about death
because you had recently

attended some severe funerals.
And you didn't want to offend,

and so developed your sense
for empathy, for couth.

What happens
when *that* shit

walks into a bar.
In the fucking pines.

On sabbatical; in the
list of ingredients
of this pantry.

In the crowd up front swaying
now uncontrollably.

People are no good.

Even as a child I had the feeling.
My grandfather tossing

a fresh nail gun cartridge
into the fire. Even then

I knew I wasn't ready.

MAMIHLAPINATAPEI

Yagan (indigenous language of Tierra del Fuego) — "the wordless, yet meaningful look shared by two people who both desire to initiate something but are both reluctant to start"

To speak of what sits in me —
rather,

to let the eyes speak. What feeds
and what grows — nursed

and so nurtured
by a stare.

To be conceived and rehearsed
silently by the iris.

No words;   not
for the lack of words, but

for the coming forth:
a tremendous journey

and too significant
a resolution.

And to angle their way
across the tongue; to make

such a trek across
the mountain of the tongue,

so finally birthed up
into air —

To initiate a presence
as they pass the throat's shapes

of resistance. The throat
and its ideologies.

But for the words to find air
just above some surface,

to come up hard
with extended necks, the words

themselves gasping, wild eyed
and red skinned,

like a boy in his summer.

For these words to fumble forth
a wet mess, a soft

but definite new fawn
into evening's blue

snow light.

But even for these words
to break and rush forth suddenly

like the most intent steed
in a cold, blind wrap

of fear, out
into the starch of January evening,

a freight of hooves
shocking and heavy across the earth

that until spring will not fully thaw —
the steed's want of virtue

as he traverses
with eyes unfixed

but fixed
to the unknowable darkness.

NYC POSTCARDS
(ONE EASTER ACROSS MCGUINNESS BLVD)

Noon mass overflows

so freezing Polack fathers kneel in the street;

the blood blue faces of their girls

are buckets of fresh milk

Na Boga ten ojciec

One holds her defective doll;

she lays it down and the eyes open,

the lashes oxidize

od Ten Syn

South Brooklyn Casket Co.

dovetails its work

for the hour everyone is found

i od Duch Swiety,

Amen

Amen.

NYC POSTCARDS (YOUR FEBRUARY TWANG)

I wanted a little something to hold.
And so make good.

Like when a woman slides
her car into a gas station

thirty miles outside
Roanoke, Virginia.

And cuts the lights,
but leaves the engine ready

and sees her skin
in that stinking overhead glow.

I want to be present,
like that.

No layer of down
for the congregation,

in my body like a rusty nail
in a jar of jelly.

*

All's well
and then that ends.

Winter plays its woodwinds.

So to speak of it,
to let it sit a minute

near the back teeth
and send it

fumbling out
into the great manicure —

(The guests get awkward,

tidy their remnants,

slouch in the kitchen.)

*

February is the curse that licks you

Softly across the jaw
And whispers pillow talk:

Go to the mirror; see for yourself.

A STOP AT THE LIGHT KEEPERS' CEMETERY

You and I drove, lost for hours
on the purposefully unsmoothed

dirt roads; I wasn't angry,
but your father's car shook apart
in the heat and dust.

We read each name
together, or I read them

to you: sweating, staring
at our ten dollar map.
Their children beneath

our feet, huddled deep
within the island clay. Ours

were still and unborn
within me. Wives were there too,

and men who once showed others
how not to go.

OH I DON'T KNOW, FIT ME ALREADY

We are seeking someone named Anthony.
He should have good references and be able

to distinguish. He should utilize brown eyes
and must not love cats, but the fact

that they're evasive, somewhere always
in the house, footing about and preying

upon each other in minor chords. Anthony's
cleanliness should be placed upon scales; however,

his patience for self-realization is no matter.
He should understand that the oath is treason,

that he will be called upon to give up succinctness.
Do you cook, Anthony? We cook.

We dabble in pulling up weeds and spending
nights without you. Once we went out late

and heard the girls say it was over, went back
inside, picked up our brooms and folded.

We can't have that again, so we ask for you.
We think about you and sit in silence some days

humming the tune. We say, he's going the distance;
for it; to break our hearts; to complete puzzles.

Anthony, we hear you on the other end of the line,
like a throat cancer patient dying to make

a last batch of crank calls. We want to say relax,
and stop the heaving. It's not all that bad, really.

What's so good about early? We should have a drink, get to
know each other, what you're looking for. Find out

that you're drafting a recourse that reads, what,
here's my plan?

WEATHER (RIGHT NOW: //   FEELS LIKE:)

An apple to peel;

sleep as sick beckoning, no revision —
a lever,

the fucking prescription.

The morning drafts: a few
lists in there

and flecks of skin ready for the city like sick confetti.

Make it good; make it nice.

The sky above all things reaches

and comes in
on a pattern of light

no less trusting than dusk
dusting our legs, saying a name

in spite of names.

Some salt;

a garden.

INDUSTRIES FOR THE BLIND OF NEW YORK STATE

Come from above
Are all in the trees

Find air in the

sound off facades
Radar of objects

This one time I found her

collapsing
a walking stick in a corner
of 57th street station

What it would be
to have a companion

on a handle

to make love always in the
tar of night

to be always a bit
under some vertigo

Did you know I put you on

that I
woke cleanly this morning

without the use of some
dawn simulator

Well I did

And the air told me
it was morning

when the little glass palace of night
shattered cleanly

and its teeth
crumbled until the sun
settled

And the yellow war
in shadows behind my face

I felt it pass

into hands and evening
like men discussing time

and the evening,

it comes long.

PORNOGRAPHY

The girls bathe deeply
and all the shape slips

beneath suds.
And the water is cupped

and spilled over arms
                    and collected again.

The girls
come clean when the water
completely spoils.

Now, your personal experience
with severe car accidents.

Sulfuric, reactive rubber,

the universe
initiating pause.

Amidst the infinite rains
the universe could see,

airbag powder is talcum. Some
allover light.

Eyes gather
to view the internal wounds

that are born beneath our knowing
but will execute the same.

YOU ARE THE MOST DIFFICULT KIND OF
HAPPINESS

Some days I wake up on a sound stage
floating out

off the pier.

It's the gait and sway;

or wanting
to crack a pill,

put a little something in the water.

Now close your eyes.

))

Close

them.

((

Your mother
moving across the living room

headed for
her death

by efficient modern kitchen.

Some vague beneath the lids light

Reductio ad absurdum.

or

Turn inward.

but keep up
on the movement.

Ears obsessed with their role: sound book
of mouth,

        pica of teeth.

No serial number;

no ser no.

        That and a nasty case

        of aplomb, a casting

    of horse cock
behind the ribcage.

What's worse?

        Bad eyes.

Now, open.

NYC POSTCARDS
(SUMMER MALAPROPOS IN THE PARK)

After a week at it

I don't write the type
of poem that floats.

Summer's been
reading Bibbins

in the patchy grass
and sweating

through my jeans.
Our white boys leave

severely even teeth marks
on their styrofoam

bud-lights and the girls
roleplay

thigh-bruised and tatted
catalog queens.

Every few minutes
we all finger

our ass-pocketed
bike locks.

Mister Softee oversees,
provides the

nickelodeon soundtrack.
Across the park

the high school boys echo
through gated

gymnasium windows
where inside the girls

are so fucking strong and just
want to be promised.

IN WIND & CITY

The campaign begins
like any other,

                    with the air cooling
like the air around a drowning,

long hawks at a distance.

Wind picks up

                 & delivers terrible acts,

acts the city's ruse.

Look, I haven't
even tried

                to describe it yet;

but from the pier
the East River churns,

the Queensborough present

       & strange *&* white.

What can I say about it.
A long crawl back,

a posturing.

And when the evening
comes pitching the night

                    every time
like a good fucking salesman,

the tide
three hundred miles

off shore begins.

The water off a body like   .

A voice off the   is   .

I want to hear you
explain it

to a child.

NYC POSTCARDS
(IN DOLLHOUSE LEATHER JACKETS)

The freezing
pre-bulimic
young models squeeze

portfolios
to their small breasts
tightly as they stalk

past the United
Cerebral Palsy of New York

at noon and all are
unsure and I emerge from

Eisenberg's
bluntly full and unwilling
to not notice
it is autumn here

in the shade
of 5th Avenue and Flatiron.

When you are in love
with the world
you cannot be too sure.

When You Are
In Love With The World

it fucking hangs out.

The two of you
fucking
hang out; and slowly,
at the pace

of acupuncture, very gently
changing

so that
if your attention
wanes,

you look around a bit
always in some new wonder.

LIGHT, A LITTLE CLARITY

I'm not sure what it was we refused but I needed to refuse it
so we went and did it together.

Me, I wanted to accelerate thickly like
heavy trucks when they carry

empty cargo containers that flail
under ropes and tie-downs.

I wanted you to take a grain of it back to the lab,

take a tall drag
off this one here and hand it back gently, see.

I wanted you

to tell me about the stench of good lake water
        drying up on the dock and how when we walked

barefoot on concrete the road stretched
away from us

so far it made us promise things unreasonable.

I wanted you to remind me of the wind picking up
        quickly from beneath its thunderhead

and the snow coming in at all angles.

At all angles,
there's light, a little clarity. All day

       I wait for it to disappear
so we might feel a little better

about the way every liquor standing back there
reminds us of someone in particular.

I have always intended to point out

the NY Police Academy students
who have given up jaywalking,

but in their eyes
want it badly

like we have it —

want it, you will say,

       like a boy on the A train
with an awkward arm around his girl, terrified if

       he's doing it right,

and terrified to let go.